Love & Other Scars

Caron Carr

Other books by this author

Love, Life, Loss (2024)

Dedication

For Shelby, my beautiful daughter.
You are my magnificent diamond.

Contents

LOVE

Love And Other Scars

Love and other scars
paint a portrait on my heart.
Love and other scars
form the landscape of my life.

Love and other scars
shape me.
Love and other scars
are who I am.

In Your Heart

I looked in your heart
And I thought I saw someone there –
a goddess, an angel…
you adore her; it shows.

If only I'd smiled
the way she's smiling now.
If only I'd shown you
how happy you made me
maybe I'd be that girl in your heart.

I looked in your heart
and I'm sure I saw someone there –
a goddess, an angel…
you love her, I know.

If only I'd listened
instead of being jealous.
If only I'd shared with you
instead of competing.

If only I'd given more,
taken less for granted.
If only I'd shown my love
a little each day.

I looked in your heart
and I knew that someone was there –
your goddess, your angel…
and that's when I cried.

I look in your heart
and I know someone's there.
'Cause when I look in your heart
I see me.

Beautiful

Wrapping me in the warmth of your love
you bathe me in comfort.

Smiling, your eyes call me beautiful
and I want to believe them.

Destiny

You are my destiny.
I see my future in your eyes.
Your kindness shelters me.
My strength is in your arms.

In you I've found everything;
my friend, my lover,
my partner
through life's adventures.

You light the darkness
and bring me joy.
The way you look at me
melts my heart.

I trust you with my heart.
You have my back.
You are my safe place.
You are my home.

You accept me.
With you I can be 'me'.
With you my heart sings.
With you I belong.

I Will Be Your Home

I'll be right by your side.
I'll be your shelter in a storm.
I can be your place to hide.
I will be your home.

Don't ever feel that all is lost.
Don't ever fear the unknown.
I will always be with you.
I will be your home.

Never wonder what comes next.
You'll never be lost in the dark.
I will always be your light.
I will be your home.

Take This Heart

Take this heart I give you
Treat it tenderly,
with care and devotion.
I beg you, keep it safe.

This heart left in your keeping
is filled with love for you.
The supply is never-ending
and the quality is true.

This heart which you now own was mine...

A Kiss Goodbye

A kiss goodbye.
When will I see you again?
Do you want me to miss you
or will I just be wasting my time?
But I can't ask it….

Please…
Don't get in that cab.
Not yet…
Please wait another moment.
But I can't say it…

So I wave.
Then I hope.
I wonder,
and I wait.
But I can't show it…

I could fall in love with someone like you

If we only had the time…

* For Fernan

Mum & Dad

Two hearts facing the unknown,
beating fears,
caring, sharing,
making dreams come true
before it's too late,
and living in love,
together.

I Love

I love:

     - rain trickling down a windowpane

     - a vivid sunset following a storm

But none bring me as much joy as you.

I love:

     - the fire of a diamond catching the sunlight

     - the sound of a stream singing its way over rocks

But nothing is as precious to me as you.

I love:

     - the feel of a newborn's hand clutching my finger

     - a rosebud opening its petals to the sun for the first time

But I love none as much as you.

Bound by Rings

The bonds of love are much too tight.
I'm suffocating beneath your wings.
Seeking freedom I'm prepared for flight,
but my hands are bound by rings.

Take back your rings and free me,
then bid me sweet goodbye.
Just tell me that you love me,
but set me free to fly.

Give me time to test my wings
until I find the moon's too high.
Maybe then I'll wear your rings,
and together we will fly.

Easier Said Than Done

What you do is tempting fate.
You know that you should leave.
You know that you should give him up...
Easier said than done.

Be glad for all the times you've shared,
stand up and walk away.
One of you must find the strength...
Easier said than done.

You know he'll never be for you.
You know you should forget him.
There's no point in hanging on...
Easier said than done.

You know the things you do are wrong,
though, at the time they feel so right.
Keep looking for answers in the stars...
Easier said than done.

All these things you know you should.
These things you'll have to do.
You know that you don't want to,
but still one day you must.

Easier said than done...
God! So much easier said than done!

Hurt

You hurt her so many times.
Then, by not fighting for her,
you hurt her most of all.

I Remember

I remember your breath on my cheek,
and your voice in my ear,
and the words and the music
as we swayed in the darkness.

I remember your eyes, happy and sad
and your lips and your smile
and your kiss in the morning
to greet each dawning day.

In my heart and in my mind, I remember.
With my ears and with my eyes, I remember.
In my dreams and every day, I remember.
But do you ever remember me?

Precious Love

Each time I see you
      is a flawless diamond
            which I enclose in the casket of my heart.

Each moment I am with you
      is a perfect pearl
            adding to the necklace of my life.

That's What Makes You 'You'

The way you roll your sleeves
and flex your forearms.
The way you lift one eyebrow
or bite your lip.

The way you glance my way
and throw your head back to laugh.
The way you tap your foot
with feigned impatience.

The way your hair flops over one eye
and how you tilt your head.
The way you say, 'hello'
and how you whisper, 'good night'.

The way you cross your arms
or how you lick your fingers.
The way you think
or how you smile.

The curl of hair peaking from your shirt
and how you run your fingers through your hair.
How you hold my hand
and lead the way.

The way you look at the ground
to hide your shy.
The way you pull me close
with a glint in your eye.

That's why I adore you.
That's what makes you 'you'.

Flaws

Like that most unique of gems, the diamond,
people too, have flaws which,
as with the diamond,
do not detract from their appeal,
but instead, serve to accentuate their beauty.

Your Last First

I want to be your last first dance,
your last first kiss.
I want to be your everything.
Will you let me be your last first?

I want to be your last first date,
your last first touch.
I want to be your girl.
Will you let me be your last first?

I want to share your last first fight,
your last first declaration of love.
I want to share your life.
Will you let me be your last first?

I want to share your last first anniversary,
your last first holiday.
I want to be your partner.
Will you let me be your last first?

It's All Your Fault

It's all your fault, you know…
I've hardly accomplished anything today.
Every time I begin something,
you creep into my thoughts –
softly, slowly at first,
and before I know it,
my imagination is filled
with thoughts of you –
warm thoughts, soft thoughts,
such loving thoughts.

But this is getting out of hand,
and I must get something done today.
So, maybe I'll begin
by doing something very important…
I'll give this to you
just to let you know
how much I want you,
how much I need you,
and how very much I love you.

I Blinked and You Were Gone

For every time you've held me
and kissed my tears away.
For all those times you said to me
"Someone stole our time today".

For all your smiles and kisses
and the memories I hold dear.
All the cuddles, hugs and wishes
which kept me safe from fear.

To lips too sad for smiling
you gave a merry tilt.
For a heart too shy for singing
you wrote a joyous lilt.

For making me feel important,
alive with joy and fun.
For bringing laughter, loud and vibrant
to a world I'd built for one.

You took my world and changed it;
made it big enough for two.
My defenses soon were rearranged.
I owe all this to you.

But I blinked,
and you were gone.

Who Better

Who better than you to understand the pain of my loneliness…

You too, are away from the one you love…

You are away from me.

What Is Left?

Tell me your story.
Show me who you are.
Lower your walls
and open your heart.

Show me your good side.
Show me your flaws.
How can I know you
if you won't let me in?

If there's no respect
or understanding
what is left
when the passion subsides?

If we don't have friendship,
if we don't have loyalty,
what is left
when the passion subsides?

If I Can't Have Everything

If I can't have everything
I'm content to be your friend.
If I can't have everything
I don't want knowing you to end.

I wouldn't want to go through life
never loving you at all.
I know I can't have all your love,
yet your smile still makes me fall
in love with you forever.

My heart is yours to treasure.

If I can't have everything
it's better than nothing at all.
If I can't have everything,
still I'll hope for you to fall
in love with me forever.

Then your heart I'll always treasure
and together, we both,
will fall in love.

Keep Walking, Walk Away

I've built a dream
that never could come true.
I've watched it fall to pieces.
Don't make me hurt again.

Keep walking, walk away.
Don't stop and don't look back.
I've said goodbye.
I can't say that word again.

Don't turn around.
Don't hesitate.
I might start running after.
Don't make me choose again.

Keep walking, walk away.
Don't stop and don't look back.
I've said goodbye.
I can't say that word again.

Don't say you'll miss me.
Just smile and say goodbye.
Then let me stand here weeping
as I watch you walk away.

Keep walking, walk away.
Don't stop and don't look back.
I've said goodbye.
I can't say that word again.

My Heart and My Head Are Wrestling

My heart and my head are wrestling
and the winner will bring pain.

My heart begs me wait for the future
but hopes and wishes may not come true.
A path to lonely nights
and the pain of loving you.

My head makes me face the here and now
and decide what I should do.
A self-inflicted loneliness
and the pain of leaving you.

My heart and my head keep wrestling
and the winner brings us pain.
Who will be the referee?
I don't want to play this game!

Running On Empty

You want me to love you
but I don't know how.
My heart's running on empty.
Love's running out now.

Don't think I'm cold hearted
with little love left,
my heart's running on empty
and I'm wary of theft.

Been hurt once too often
by words that cut deep.
My heart's running on empty,
no love left to keep.

Hold Me Without Talking

Hold me without talking

Just hold me tight
and keep me safe
'till morning.
Protect me with your arms.

Maybe we won't make it together
but just for one night
let's pretend we can,
while you hold me without talking.

I don't need promises.
You don't need to say you care.
Just hold me close,
hold me without talking.

Wrap your arms around me.
Let me lay my cheek to your chest
so I can hear your heart beating
as you hold me without talking.

Something Sad

There's something sad about us;
we can't live together
but we can't live apart.

Whenever I leave
you cry a little inside.
When you say goodbye
 my sadness is hard to hide.

There's something sad about us
I can't live with you
and I die when we're apart

There's something sad about us
I can't live without you
and you can't live with me

There's something sad about love
when all it brings is hurt.

When, Suddenly

'Twas not my plan to fall for you.
'Twas not my wish but by decree.
Some master plan to disturb my life
did pull me from my safety nest
and thrust me into love's fine mess.

For years I wandered,
no care for which direction.
My life chose to follow.
When suddenly, I caught a star.

For years I was lonely.
Not reaching for friendship,
I trusted no-one.
When suddenly, I touched a rainbow.

For years I was pain free.
Not letting myself be vulnerable,
my heart was far from reach.
When suddenly, I saw the wind.

Not now for me those days of fear,
loneliness and sorrow.
Scoffing at thoughts of warmth and love,
putting up fences should someone come near.

For you, my love, gave me rainbows,
handed me stars and showed me the wind.
You, my love, have killed my fear.
For you, my love and heart is here.
Do with them what you will.

Where Are You Now?

Where are you now my love?
Do you ever wonder where I am?
I loved you enough to let you go
but I couldn't say goodbye.
Easier by far to disappear
and try to right the wrongs.
But the agony of tears
has left a chasm in my heart.
On the outside I've forgotten,
inside the hurting grows and grows.

If, by chance, you hear my heart,
hear it reaching out to yours,
if your heart's still there for me
then my whole world is you.

You and I

We've seen a lot, you, and I,
and not without regrets.
We've shared each other's torment
and guarded one another's secrets.

We've been through much, you and I,
to each our share of pain.
I felt the hurt you suffered
while you helped to keep me sane.

We're not alone, you and I.
Our hearts have both been broken.
But we've seen each other through,
often with thanks unspoken.

We've calmed each other's heartbreak
and felt each other's pain.
We still hold each other's secrets
but we're the ones who've gained.

I know we always had it.
It just took some time to bloom.
It's not the love we sought.
but we've found friendship, you and I.

The Reflections Of Our Love

Think about me…
Think about you…
What about us?
What about the love we shared?
Don't you love me as you did
or don't you love me any more?
What happened to end *us*?
You and me?... We?
What happened to all our thoughts,
our ideas, our plans, our unity?
Where did it all go wrong?
Where did *we* all go wrong?
Dear God, what happened?

Our love was a lifetime investment,
slowly grown from infancy into maturity,
cultivated and cared for,
but at the same time sudden and strange,
war, safe and sheltering,
but frightening and unveiling.
What became of that investment?
Blown up, destroyed,… crippled and maimed,
rejected and ignored.
That love now cold and threatening
drives me to my knees.

But we were sure to have such fun,
children, a home, holidays, success and more…
love ever after, for good, of for bad…
You said you loved me,
said we were made as a pair,
just like Siamese twins.
How can you turn and walk away
from the things we would have done.

Don't you see?
　　　I'm pleading with you.
Can't we try again?
　　　We once had the magic.
Oh, *please* let's try again.
The reflections of our love won't hurt us again.
Those reflections have hurt us too much in the past.
I'll never let their rebounds destroy or defeat us
So *please*, let's try just once more.

For Him

Two hearts
bound together in the dance of life.
One heart skips a beat,
the music ceases,
and the rhythm stops.
One heart dances alone
in the shadows
and remembers.

Let It Rain

You've gotta let it rain
for at least a day or more
'cause after the tears
have washed away the pain
you'll be free,
free to love again.

Step by step
feel your way,
bit by bit
take it day by day.

It takes a little time
to heal the wounds of love.
Just find a little patience
and storms will turn to sunshine.
One day, your sun will shine again.

Best Friends

Can't you see I *want* to be more than your best friend?
Can't you see I *need* to be more than your best friend?
Can't you see I'll *never* be just your best friend?

A kiss hello is very nice,
but my needs run much deeper.
I don't want to discuss the weather.
I just want us to be together.

I'll always know
exactly what I'm missing
so I can't spend a lifetime
keeping my emotions hidden.

If you want me to fake friendship
when really, I want more,
I don't think I can ever cope
with being your best friend.

When I'm With You

I can see sunshine in the dark,
I can feel songs in the wind
when I'm with you.

I hear the sun shining through a storm,
I can smell raindrops in the desert
when I'm with you.

Miracles surround you,
Goodness walks your footsteps.
All is good with the world
when I'm with you.

No Warning

No warning, I just sensed that we were through.
Don't know how, but I just knew.

When did the fire stop raging?
How can I fan the spark again?
Why did the sunshine fade to night?
Who stole the rainbow from my days?
Did anybody see when the hope fled from my dreams?

Seems now we're two streams flowing to different seas.
Now we're just two hearts, one flying away from each other.

Suddenly the smile slipped from your eyes,
and the flowers were no longer in your arms.
All the tenderness left your hands.
It was time for us to end.

Guess we're just two lives falling apart at the seams.
Seems now we're two lovers dreaming different dreams.

One couple tearing each other apart.

This Torment Inside Me

You say we are surely soul-mates
yet our love just cannot be.
Can't you feel how much my heart aches
when you smile and glance my way.

You treat me as a lover
though we must just be friends.
What do you want from me?
When will this all end?

I try to tell my heart
that you don't mean a thing
but you reach for my heart
and teach it how to sing.

Been waiting patiently
to know just how you felt.
Now you've said you care for me
what a cruel hand fate has dealt.

We shouldn't be together.
I should just say goodbye,
think of you each day, forever
and pray our love will die.

You have someone else to think of.
You belong to them, not me.
So, treasure all the love
it takes to set you free.

I'll walk out in the snow,
crying tears you'll never see
and no-one else will ever know
this torment inside me.

Tomorrow

All too soon tomorrow becomes yesterday
and today fast becomes the past.
Tomorrow has come too quickly
and yesterday is but a memory.

Will tomorrow ever be today for us?
Will today ever be the past?
Will yesterday ever become a memory of us?
Or, is tomorrow just another fleeting dream?

* For Fernan

I Would Do Anything

I would do anything
to see your smiling eyes.
Cross the wildest oceans
to fall asleep wrapped in your arms.

I would do anything
to share your dreams.
Climb the highest mountains
to walk beside you through your life.

I would do anything
for your love.

Two Hearts Lost

Two hearts sharing the same path
down the track, narrow and winding.

as the trees close in upon them,
one lags, losing sight of the other.

At a junction different directions.

Two hearts
…lost.

Wishing Hurts Away

I've tried hard not to love you,
I know it shouldn't be.
But you know I've grown to love you
just as I know that you love me.

I know I've never told you
just how much I care
but you've looked deep into my eyes
and the words are written there.

Don't think that I don't love you
because the words are left unsaid.
You know how much I love you
by the things I do instead.

At night I lay awake and dream
of the things I want to say,
but all my courage disappears.
when you look at me that way.

When you beg me not to love you
you're just wishing hurts away.
We both worry about tomorrow
but we'll still enjoy today.

Without Him Now

I've lived without him before
and never longed for more.
Now I long for happiness.
Why can't I live without him now?

Long ago, without him, I would sleep.
Now, all I do is dream and weep;
dreams full of loss and emptiness.
Why can't I sleep without him now?

I can't because I love him.
I love him so much it hurts.
Things change at love's sweet whim,
and to this you must be alert.

When you're with someone
you never appreciate
that you're truly happy and contented,
at peace and fulfilled,
until something unexpected
wreaks havoc with your world.
I love you and I miss you.
Come home soon.

I See You

I see your short comings,
your faults,
I smell your weakness,
your insecurities.
I feel your moods,
your quirks and habits,
your ups and downs.
I touch your vulnerability.
I feel your wounds,
your melancholy.
I hear your mistakes.
I don't love you despite them.
I love you *because* of them.
I see you.

Flowers

Don't bring me flowers
when you're sorry.
Don't bring me flowers
when I'm sad.

The best time to bring me flowers
Is for no reason, no reason at all.

Don't tell me you love me
when I'm feeling lonely.
Don't tell me you love me
when I'm upset.

The best time to say you love me
is for no reason,
no reason except that you do.

Loss

Have I lost you
or just the hopes and dreams,
the future that I linked to you?

Did I ever really have you?

Did that future ever really exist?

Better Without You

The moon was broken,
the sun in shatters,
rivers stopped flowing
and mountains dissolved
because you took your love away.
Music was silenced,
art in ashes,
my life in disarray
when you took your love away.

You made me feel so much less,
so great a nothing
but that was wrong.
It is you who are less,
you who is nothing..
You deserve nothing from me.
You will get nothing from me.
I am better without you.

If I Should Stay

If I should stay
will I end up broken hearted?

If I should stay
will I thank my lucky stars
will you treat me right
If I should stay.

If I should stay
will you hold me in your heart.
Will I find it all with you
if I should stay.

Unsaid

I can't live with the words I left unsaid.
Everything is such a mess.
Nothing has become what it should.
You won't believe the words I left unsaid.

I swallowed my pride
but it's killing me that you'll never know
the words I left unsaid.

They say things happen for a reason.
I guess this is how it's meant to be
and it's right that you'll never know
the words I left unsaid.

Just as I'll never know
the words you left unsaid...

All Said And Done

All said and done,
at the end of the day,
I love you.

You make me smile,
you make me whole,
you get me.
All I know
is that you're my person.
You make things right.

All said and done
when you know, you know
and all said and done
at the end of the day,
I love you.

It's not a dream,
not something imagined.
So very real,
so very good.

All said and done,
it's something I want.
All said and done,
at the end of the day,
I love you.

Distance

Even when you are with me
you aren't really there.

I talk to you but you never hear;
never seem to understand.

Do you feel empty on the inside too?

Time

Drinks, bright lights,
loud music, and a hot night.
Soft hands, slow kisses 'till dawn.
Now it's time for me to go.

Good times, heated fights,
a home shared,
and dreams crushed.
Now it's time for me to go.

Decades lived, children raised,
a lifetime of love.
Strength fading, spirit weakening.
Now it's time for me to go.

A Gift

Every day with you is a gift.

My tomorrows are yours to give.

Eternal Love

True love never dies,
not in our hearts.
Time steals our looks,
even our lives away, but it cannot steal our love.
The conscious mind acknowledges
the constant passing of time.

Seasons come and go.
We age, we perish.
In our hearts we are immortal.
We yearn for beauty, truth,
and meaning in our lives.
A part of us yearns for something better.

Once we find love, we become Eternal.

Life Isn't Easy

Life isn't always beautiful.
The world is sometimes cruel.
But life's beautiful around you.
In my life you are the jewel.

Hardships come and go.
Sadness floods my heart.
Yet you take all the sorrow.

Love

Love spans the miles,
stretching across the mountains,
reaching across the oceans,
defying all concepts of time,
finding its victims.

Love has walked this earth
since this world was created.
Like a disease
it has rested and waited
just around every corner
waiting to claim its prey,
waiting to exert its power,
the power to control the world;
the power to tame its opponents.

Love tames even the most powerful of beasts.
Love exists in the farthest corner of the universe.
It has no limits, no confines.
It feeds and multiplies in the hearts of lovers.
Each time its victims fall in love
its power is two-fold.
Love is indestructible.
Even death has no effect on love.
Love has always Been.
And love will still Be;
even when life is gone.

* First published in 'SPECTRUM, An International Poetry Anthology', 1982

You Saw

I saw the here and now,
this moment;
scared to look ahead.

But you saw the whole.
You saw the rest of our lives.

Let Not Love

Let not love be bound by shackles
which tie two lives as one,
restricting individuality
like a barrier before a racehorse.

Let love draw you together
while you exist alone
just as the strings of a cello
must be plucked alone;
yet the song is the same
that makes them sing.

Let not love become the pillow
smothering hopes and dreams.
Instead create from love
a blanket of caring.

As trees stand apart
yet together form a forest
let love give you strength
to stand apart as one.

Stand together in love
but let not love make you
exclusive unto yourselves.

Let not love become a cage
cutting you off from liberty.
Rather, let love be that box
containing your soul
which you give freely
to those deserving of it.

Give of your love
without conditions or strings.

Donate it often and ask nothing in return.
Then, when love is returned to you,
you'll harvest its rewards with interest.

Let love become the gateway to release,
the window to freedom and contentment.
Let not love make you an kraken
crushing your loved one in its tentacles.
Let not love be the string
which binds you to another.
Instead, let love be a gift of freedom.

Work together as one, but not too close.
For the pylons on a bridge
must stand apart ,
and a rose cannot bloom
within the shadow of the willow.

Let love be in you
and you will always live with love.

What Price Love

How much to build a memory?
How much is it worth?

Days of love and affection,
and knowing someone cares.
Roses on the doorstep
and candles on the table,
stolen kisses in the darkness
and glances across the room,
moonlit strolls down beaches
and running in the rain.
Lovemaking in a grassy field
and cuddling in a storm,
winters spent by fireside,
hopes and dreams exchanged,
strong arms hold my tears
and cradle me when I sleep…
What cost these memories?
What is it that I risk?
How much are they worth?
A little bit of pain?

Yes, willingly!

His Eyes

His eyes,
they cut me like a knife.
They reach deep into my soul
to learn what's hidden there.

Our Moon

I know you're out there listening
waiting for a voice to call your name.
I know you're out there looking
and I'm looking just the same.

Somewhere out there
if you can see the moon,
know that I'm here wishing on it
praying I can find you soon.

Don't stop searching for me.
Keep gazing on our moon.
Though the way is long and lonely
I know we'll find each other soon.

There were times I though I'd found you.
Seems I always got it wrong.
Have to keep on searching.
It's with you that I belong.

You

I love you dearly
        as the grass loves the oak tree
            at whose feet it rests.

As the rose needs dew
        to bless its morning splendor,
            so do I need you.

All I Have Is Me

I could give you a pot of gold
or a yacht to sail the sea
but they'll mean nothing when we're old,
so, all I have for you is me.

I could write you love songs,
clothe you in silk, and fine jewelry.
But all that sparkles won't last long,
and all I have for you is me.

So much I'd like to give you
but few things come for free.
Accept this gift I give to you,
it comes with love from me.

Two Hearts

Two hearts emerging from the shadows;
intrepid explorers on an emotional trail
dwarfed by trees of uncertainty.
Touched by sunshine,
two hearts kissed by love.

Home Is Where The Heart Is

Home is where the heart is
and I left my heart with you.
As I walked through your door
my heart chose to remain.

Treat it kindly dear,
protect it with your love.
Because home is where the heart is
and my heart is in your care.

Nurture it and tend it
with all the love you have.
Nurse it as a baby
for slowly as it grows
you'll come to know the love I feel
grows stronger as it flows.

Love knows not the miles between us
and will never grow to wane
because you're my home and shelter.
Your love saves me from the pain.

Loneliness

Even loneliness it beautiful
with the right person sharing it.

So Hard

It's so hard to say goodbye to us.

We had the future.
We had forever.
Now, that's all in the past,
all in the never,
killed by a thousand paper cuts.

It's so hard to say goodbye,
and even harder to move on.

Love's First Touch

As the mountains welcome winter's first snow flakes
their landing slow and peaceful,
and as spring greets the first jonquil blooms,
their golden beauty warming winter's gloom,
so, will I welcome love's first touch.

Heads upturned for mother's feast
squawking their eagerness for her gifts
the eagle's chicks are all waiting her return.
I too await love's sweet awakening.

A young child learning to walk,
tottering its way to a mother's skirts.
I too will reach out for love's attentions.

As a stream winds its way into a river's arms,
so, will I be clasped in love's warm embrace.

I will be loved.

Vacation

I take a vacation from reality when I'm with you.

Everything Hurts

Everything hurts;
every little thing,
everyday things,
every part of me....
hurts.

But days come and go,
the moon rises and falls,
bearing the pain, I will go on...
without you.

Two Minutes Ten Seconds

Two minutes and ten seconds
is how long it took you
to tell me it was over.
Two minutes and ten seconds
to eradicate us.
Two minutes and ten seconds
for you to kill tomorrow.

Chances Are

Chances are I am about to lose
yet I dive right in
arms open, heart full of hope
head pushing away doubts,
to try again;
chasing life's ultimate prize;
a future filled with dreams,
tomorrows full of possibilities,
and a life shared with you

Let's Dance

An admiring bow,
one hand taking another
gliding onto the dancefloor
playing it cool.

Step, 2, 3.
Back, 2, 3.
Work it out 2, 3.
Dance, 2, 3.

Dancing as one.
We cannot stop
what has begun;
this dance of love.

You Do You

You do you.
I'll do me
and together
we'll do us
together as we.

Whatever

If ever you should…
Whenever you need…
Should you ever feel…
Wherever you might…
If you ever want…
However you may…
Whenever you fear…
If there's ever anything….
No matter what…
Whatever happens…
I'll be there with you.

A Cup Of Tea

When they met he took her dancing,
saved his pennies for phone calls,
and planned the future.

He brings her a cup of tea to greet the morning
and kisses to bid the day goodnight.

Children came and grew to adults
his every decision was discussed with her.
His every thought shared.

He brings her a cup of tea to greet the morning
and kisses to bid the day goodnight.

He always knew the cards in the hand she held.
Could read it in her twinkling eyes.
He chased her with a pitchfork;
she kept the photo to prove it.
She pranked him every chance she got.

He brings her a cup of tea to greet the morning
and kisses to bid the day goodnight.

As she got sicker his love showed stronger,
his work-hardened hands tender and gentle
as he sat at her side watching her drift away.

He brings her a cup of tea to greet the morning
and kisses to bid the day goodnight.

She left him for Heaven many years ago
but still he brings her a cup of tea to greet the morning
and kisses to bid the day goodnight.

Choice

Who are we without the ability to choose?
I choose love.
I choose you.
I choose us.

To Love One's Enemy

She's a hun and Tom's a pom.
They didn't mean to do no wrong.
They're torn between the worlds of love and war,
each locked in the other's gloom.
Will he live or will he die
in that craft he has to fly?
her brother bombs old London Town
while Tom shoots Berlin's bridges down.
She half expects them both to die at once
shot down by the other's gun.
Who'll be to blame she doesn't know
'cause that would spoil the whole damn show
and she could never fact the thought again.

The letter came one misty day
and it still fails to explain
how his plain was forced to ditch,
diving down into the sea.
Parachute all torn to shreds,
tumbling to the deep, blue, deep,
hitting with an enormous splash,
dead before he even hit.
Crumpled bones, a crippled mess.
Buried in a foreign grave.
She won't even morn or even cry
because it is against the rules,
to love one's enemy.

* First published in 'SPECTRUM, An International Poetry Anthology', 1982

All I See Is You

I look in his eyes
I see you.
I'm kissing his lips
I feel you.

A guy passes my door
I see you.
Someone drives by me.
All I see is you.

A song on the radio
I think of you.
The touch of someone's hand
I feel you.

My eyes are blind to others
I see you.
I can't get you off my mind.
All I see is you,
Always you.

Messy

Love is messy
filled with misunderstandings,
flooded with insecurities,
overflowing with uncertainties,
clumsy and tripping,
minds meeting and clashing
on equal terms,
confusing and inconvenient,
definitely a bumpy road.
Love is a risk
and rarely easy.

Jump in anyway,
travel that road,
untangle the knots,
give love a chance,
and get dirty.
Let's take a risk on love.

In Your Eyes

In your eyes
is a world of love.
Your touch
embodies kindness.
Your smile
spreads happiness.
Your hug
holds me safe.
Your words
are filled with care.
You represent all that is good,
kind, and wonderful.
You make me feel good enough.
You make me feel worthy.
May I do the same for you.

For Fernan

It's been nine long days
since I watched that taxi drive away
and as that vehicle became smaller
it took my heart and you from me.

From time to time you come
tiptoeing into my thoughts.
You stop, take my hand, and kiss me.
You lean dreamily against the door
eyes moist as you watch me walk away.
Your eyes caress my back.
I can feel them.
I want to look back and catch your gaze
but don't for fear you've disappeared.
I take a breath and turn.
You wave and blow a kiss.

Yesterday I heard you whisper in my ear
"I am the coffee and you are the cream".
Memories triggered by a song.
You, singing softly in the dark,
dancing me around in a dream of our own,
wishing the night would never end.
I treasure the memories.
Untold value in each one.

Today another taxi left the kerb
and peering through the window of my mind
was your disappearing face.
So much left unsaid.
I wander aimlessly from day to day.
In my mind, that night didn't end....

The Silence

See this instrument of torture.
It bears witness to your lies.
"I want you to feel special" you said.
"I just want you to feel my love",
"Our meeting was so fortuitous" you declared.

Yet the silence mocks your sincerity.
"We'll do this and we'll do that"
Ah, the grandest dreams!
"I want to talk to you often
and know you warts and all".
Bah! The silence justifies my cynicism.
This instrument of torture rests mute.
Another day and still you do not call.

Two Hearts

Two hearts
bound together in the dance of life.

One heart skips a beat,
the music ceases
and the rhythm stops.

One heart
dances alone in the shadows
and remembers the song.

Don't Wake Me Up

If this is a story
don't let it end.
If this is a myth
let me live it.
If this is a book
let me keep turning the pages.
If this is a song
don't stop singing.
If this is a dream
Don't wake me up.

Everything is inside-out
upside down and back to front
but I wouldn't have it
any other way.
If this is a dream
Don't wake me up.

I Lay Me Down

It's raining in my heart
and I'm drowning in my tears.
Just when I think I'm over you
memories tear my heart to shreds.

I have a pocket full of memories
with no-one around to share.
Your face has become an etching
within the gallery of my mind.

My heart aches when I see you
and when I think of times we shared
I just lay me down and cry me off to sleep.
Every night I hunger for your love.
I long to hold your warn and tender body close to mine.
My heart aches every time I think of you.
You brought the seeds of love
and planted them in my heart.

I wish there'd been more time
in which to share our love.
You never said "I love you".
I could have made love right and real.
I'll always be here waiting
should you ever need a friend,
and I always will be willing
To lend a helping hand.

Perhaps I was a fool
to hope you really cared.
And maybe I'm a fool
still loving you as I do,
but, if dreams are what they say,
then our lives will touch again.
In the meantime, I'm still hoping

because Heaven is lonely without you.
Again I'll lay me down and cry me off to sleep.

What Is It?

What is it,
that gives me a warm glow
whenever you hold me close?

How is it,
you can make me feel
so happy and complete?

I have no idea… but you do.

Why do I love you?
Don't ask me why…
I just know I do.

Why is it,
I want nothing more
than to spend
every day through my life
walking beside you?

I have no idea… But I do,
and I will.

Home Is Where the Heart Is

Home is where the heart is
and I left my heart with you.
As I walked through your door
my heart chose to remain.
Treat it kindly, dear.
Protect it with your love.
Because home is where the heart is
and my heart is in your care.

Nurture it and tend it
with all the love you have.
Nurse it as a baby; for slowly as it grows,
you'll come to know the love I feel
grows stronger as it flows.
Love knows not the miles between us
and will never begin to want.
Because you're my home and shelter.
Your love saves me from life's pain.

Because

Because you are the rest of my life.
Because you are the reason I live.
Because you are the reason I am.

Because you are my breath and my blood.
Because you are every thought in my mind.
Because you are everything.

The Life and Death of a Rose

With help from winds and sunshine
the smallest seed is sown.

I met you long ago
and we felt we'd met before.

Caressed by earth and rain,
a tiny leaf begins to show.
For time unmeasured, no one sees it change.
As it grows from shrub to bush,
strangers rush by without a glance
never guessing what they miss.

Gradually, over weeks and months,
a friendship slowly grew.
As we were drawn together
we discovered feelings growing too.

With the coming of the Spring,
a bud begins to form.
Time swells delicate petals within
'till a flash of colour peeps between the green.

We kept our feelings hidden,
both from each other and the world.
When your first kiss stirred emotions
I thought the world would see.

Within a day, the bloom, newly opened,
is draped in diamonds kissed by the sun's first rays.

You loved me for the first time
and still the world was blind.
Our love remained a secret
locked up within our hearts.

One rose followed by another
placed in a vase to enjoy.
Then another, and another,
and I pray there will be more.

Each time you held or kissed me
was a moment blessed by love.
A rare and valued treasure
for no one else to see.

My body feels a shiver
as a gust blows through the door.
Nothing lives forever;
the first petal hits the floor.

The forbidden love we shared
bore with it happiness and sorrow,
a yearning for what I wanted most,
yet knew could never last.

I empty out the vase
and toss away the stems.
I stoop to gather all the petals
and hold them for a while.
I savor their sweet perfume
then softly start to cry.
I bathe them with my teardrops
but tomorrow I must smile.
I'll keep them with my memories
buried beside forbidden love.

Love waited, hidden by the shadows,
'till no one was around,
then together we picked the roses
which no one else had seen.
We stole those fleeting moments

where no one else belonged.
Our love may have been forbidden
but for us the roses bloomed!

Faeries Are Real

I know that
faeries are real
and love is not a state of mind.
Love is real.

Dreams are dreams
but only if you let them be.
Chase a dream
and it becomes reality.

I know that
faeries are real
and love is not a state of mind.
Love is real.

Games are games
but only if you want them to be.
Play the game
and it becomes reality.

I know that
faeries are real
and love is not a state of mind.
Love is real.

So don't tell me faeries
are just a state of mind
or that love is never real.
I've seen both and...

I know that Faeries are real
and love is not a state of mind
Love is real.
Love's so real it hurts.

For Elaura

And so I lay me down again
to cry myself to sleep.
Maybe tears will end my pain.
Come a time when I'll no longer weep.

With every breath I take
I pray time will heal my heart.
But should it break before I wake
and thus, my soul depart,
know that happily I give my life
to the memory of loving you.

For you are gone before me,
to a place devoid of pain,
and I live my life in misery
'till I can love with you again.

Prisoner of Dreams

There was a dream,
somewhere inside my head.
There was such love,
spilling from my heart.

Hope springing from a word,
growing with the flash of a smile.
Life built on a fantasy.
Love born on a breeze.

Crystals… tossed and shattered.
Rainbows… beaten and battered.
Stolen moments full of teardrops,
filling an ocean of loneliness.

You were that dream,
somewhere inside my head.
You were that love,
spilling from my heart.

You held my fate.
You were the rest of my life.

What Color Is Your Love?

What color is your love?
Red; burning with heat,
a yellow glow,
dark with intensity,
pink of newborn innocence
or a rainbow of everything?

What We Cannot Change

This time I won't fall for love.
No, it'll never happen again.
This time there'll still be stars above.
I'll see the sunshine through the rain.

You see, I know you'll be gone one day
just as a leaf lost to the wind.
I'll hurt for just a moment
but everything has its end.

Nothing stays the same forever.
Nothing's made to withstand change.
Though the stars never seem to alter
through the seasons they rearrange.

I thought that you were only
bringing comfort to a friend.
You're there when I am lonely
but I know that we will end.

Life's a gamble for you and I
so don't be afraid to bet.
Learn to live with a life of change,
and what we cannot change, accept.

Where Are You Now My Love?

Where are you now, my love?
Am I ever in your thoughts?
Do you carry 'round my photograph?
Does it ever hurt to say my name?
Have you ever set an extra place
in the hope that I'd be back?
How long before you believed I'd really gone?

Do you ever look for me?
When you see red hair shining in the sun
do you expect to see my face?
At night do you still dream of me?
Do you wake and reach for me
to find someone else instead?
And do another's arms feel wrong?

Have you ever wanted to call me
just to hear me say 'hello'?
And every time your phone rings
does your heart still skip a beat?

Where are you now, my love?
Do you ever think of me?
And have you ever wondered
if I ever think of you?

I Promise You

If ever you are lonely
and in need of a friend,
I promise you,
I'll be there.

When the world outside
gets too intense,
I promise you,
I'll be your shield.

When you're feeling abandoned
by all around you,
I promise you,
I'll be at your side.

If every moment feels tough
and you want to give up,
I promise you,
I'll take the load.

If you feel weak,
or are feeling afraid,
I promise you,
I'll be your courage.

When you feel despair,
if you ever feel down
I promise you,
I'll be around.

If you're falling apart,
finding it hard to cope,
I promise you,
I'll be your glue.

When days are dark,
and all around is stormy,
I promise you,
I'll be your shelter.

If every minute is a struggle
when everything hurts,
I promise you,
I'll be your strength.

When the wind blows cruel
and people don't care
I promise you,
I'll be your kindness.

when life is kind,
filled with times to celebrate,
I promise you,
I'll be your party.

Lock The Door

Go inside and lock the door.
Shut me out,
don't let me in.
Keep your walls up,
don't let them in.
Love is scary.
Love can't be trusted.
Love can be deceiving.
Go inside and lock the door.
Shut everyone out,
don't let anyone in.
Don't say the lock is broken.
Don't tell me where you hide the key.
Go inside and lock the door.
Shut the world out.

Write You A Song

I want to write you a song.
I want to tell you what you mean to me.
I want you to see how much I love you.
I want you to know you're everything.

I want to write you a song.
My pen scratches on the page.
My fingers pluck at the strings.
My words are shaped by love for you.

I want to write you a song.
I hum the melody of my love.
I sing my words of praise.
I pour my heart into this song for you.

I want to write you a song.
I need you to know you are special.
I need to tell you you are precious.
I need you to know you are beautiful.

Love In Glass Houses

Everyone has an opinion.
Advice and criticism left and right.
Stones thrown.
Sticks hurled.

Love in glass houses
in full view of the world,
audience at the ready.
Critics amass at the fence line.

Speculation and assumptions.
Everyone else knows best.
You should.
You shouldn't.

Love in glass houses.
No protection.
No privacy.
No room for errors.

OTHER SCARS

Broken

Held on for too long,
forced to be strong
until I unravelled.

Demons torture
torn from rapture
until I shattered

Fail after fail
holding on with tooth and nail
going off the rails.

Hour to hour, day to day
always a price to pay
until I'm properly broken.

I Don't Cry Pretty

Crying leaves its mark on me;
blotchy skin and blood shot eyes,
nose blocked up and stuffy.
I don't cry pretty.

Childhood rumble
I took a tumble,
skinned my knee.
I don't cry pretty.

Teenage sweethearts,
mixed up, torn apart,
heartbreak city.
I don't cry pretty.

Wedding bells,
a day of tears
and confetti.
I don't cry pretty.

A brand new life
cradled in my arms,
so precious and tiny.
I don't cry pretty.

A lifetime lived,
gone in a moment,
a loss felt deeply.
I don't cry pretty.

For Sharon

I'm such a long way away
but I'm here.
I think of you often
and wish you were near.
When you're in trouble
I worry,
and when you're happy
I'm glad.
Whenever you need me,
I'm here.
I'm your friend.

I'm Not

You say that I'm strong
but I'm not, so very not.

Life is tough.
It tears me down and beats me up.
I struggle every day;
can't seem to find the way.

There are times I can't go on
and want to give up
but still I step into the fray;
keep going anyway.

I spend my life pretending.
I just fake it a lot.
Make as though I'm coping
while all the time I'm panicking.

Weakness overwhelms me
makes it hard to function.
Emotions right and raw
urge me to withdraw.

You say that I'm strong
but I'm not, so very not.

One Tear

Watery glaze fills the eye
swelling and forming one glassy pearl;
pools atop the bottom lid,
trembling, quivering on the brink
until it spills over,
topples to create on glittering diamond
trickling down the cheek,
reaching for the jaw.
Pauses, then drips into nowhere.
A single tear
followed closely by another
and another;
a storm of tears
releasing an ocean of pain.

Don't Give Up On You

Don't give up on you,
hold on tight and don't let go.
You will make it through.

It isn't over, it isn't done,
keep on trying.
Keep looking for the sun.

I know you think you're weak.
I know you're tired.
But you're stronger than you think.

Days are tough,
and you feel alone.
This will be over soon enough.

Old Friend Fig Tree

Draped in fog,
or bathed in sunshine,
old friend fig tree stands in majesty,
branches outstretched, embracing the sky.

The bird chorus greets the new dawn.
Busy birds, come and going all day,
season by season,
tending their young.

Leaves whisper in a breeze
and roar through a storm,
moss on branch and trunk
vividly green in the rain.

Late afternoon brings lorikeets and cockatoos
gathering for their afternoon party,
loud and squabbling
over the feast of fruits.

Shade for horses,
nests for birds,
and homes for rabbits in the tangle of roots.
Trunk and leaves glow gold as the sun sets.

Silhouetted against the twilight,
a possum family runs along the branches
of the possum highway.
Old friend fig tree, I will miss you.

Happiness

Happiness isn't 'out there' somewhere.
It's not something to wait for
nor something to look for.
Happiness is hiding behind every sadness.
Happiness is inside us all waiting to be aroused.
Happiness is right here, right now

Mum

The sky shed a tear
as I lay a rose
beside your resting head
moments after you left.

The skies turned gloomy
and the days were dark.
Nothing is the same
without you in my world.

Moments filled with nothing,
heart filled with emptiness,
life goes on without you
every second a struggle.

I hate that you left so early;
that you've missed so much of my journey
I must keep sailing
across the ocean of life
with its becalming winds
and smashing storms,
sailing without you,
alone with my dragons
and a chalice filled with sorrow.

Home

Home isn't always where the heart is,
Sometimes home *is* the heart.

Human

I'm only human
with my full complement of flaws
along with skills and assets,
worries, frustrations, joys, and dreams.

I'm only human,
perfectly normal,
perfectly human.

She

She was shy
but tried not to show it,
with insecurities
and angst.
She was lost,
adrift on the sea of life.
She knew she was a misfit
but tried so hard to fit in.
Sad and depressed,
masking it with comedy.
She was kind,
sensitive and naïve.
She was bookish and clever,
bad at sports but nerdy.
She was young.
She was innocent.
She was somebody I used to know.
She was somebody I used to be.

Demons

The demons within me
want to lash out
and crush your soul.

The demons within me
need to lash you with my tongue.

The demons within me
hurls words like swords
to pierce your heart.

The demons within me
long to hurt you
as much as you've hurt me.

The demons within me
condemn me relentlessly
for feeling this way.

Louder

Nothing shouts louder
than the silence of loneliness.

The Heart Of Our Land

With sun drenched beaches,
fertile, lush plains,
soaring mountains and harsh deserts
all born from the dreaming.

Cities new and landscapes old,
animals unique and birds
bright with color and chatter.
Wattle and gums dot the skyscape.

Raging storms, blistering summers,
ravaging bushfires devouring all in their path.
Seeds explode and vegetation is reborn.
In the west a carpet of wildflowers.

Big skies, endless plains,
rolling hills, rugged mountains,
harsh coastlines, endless beaches
and the red, red dirt of the outback.

Mateship part of our DNA,
'she'll be right', a 'can do' attitude,
and, we all 'ava go' not just in sport
but in life as well.

From the green gums to the golden wattles
this great land down south,
the heart of our land
Our land, Australia.

Rules

Who makes the rules?
Who decided red and green should never be seen together?

Who decided what is 'normal' and what is not?
Who says what must be?

Who determined that left is left and right is not?
Who decides what is right or wrong?

Who decided the 'proper' way to drink tea?
Who decided these are the rules?

Who decided that red is for stop and green for go?
Who decides the way we live?

Tell me, who decides…

This Too, Shall Pass

You are an angel who forgot how to fly,
a fairy who lost her wand.
You've lost the way forward
and don't know how to carry on.
Something is broken deep inside you,
crushed and shattered into pieces.

It's a tragedy,
Don't give up.
You are not broken,
crushed or shattered.

Don't fret.
You are stronger than you know;
resilience in every pore.
Get ready for the fight of your life.
Get ready to fight for your life.

You are perfectly human
in an imperfect world.
This too, shall pass.
This is your time,
time to shine.

Once more, you will fly over mountains,
see the world at your feet.
Again, you will find yourself.
Once again, you will heal.

This Is The World

Loneliness in all our cities,
communities broken apart.
Where are the villages that raise our children?
This is the world we have created.

Violence at every turn,
war in every corner
and people shouting hate.
This is the world we have created.

Children living in poverty,
starvation all around.
Does anyone really care?
This is the world we have created.

Our earth depleted,
our seas polluted,
animals facing extinction.
This is the world we have created.

Deeds

No deed is too small.
No deed is pointless.
No deed stays unnoticed.
Every deed matters.

Smile at a stranger,
help your neighbor,
reach out to someone
lend a helping hand
mark each day with
an unexpected kindness.

Let's build a world of deeds;
a better world,
a kinder world.

Your Forever Friend

Every time you meet someone
it seems we drift apart.
We no longer stop to sit and talk.
I just don't know where to start.

And, you, my friend
begin to think
I no longer understand.
Our friendship's on the brink.

I guess I feel unneeded.
At times it seems I don't belong.
I'm lonely and neglected.
Please show me I am wrong.

We've known each other so many years
and never disagreed.
Why then, do we find it so easy
to let dissention sow its seed?

I guess our friendship just gets lazy
when we don't speak honestly.
Though there's someone else who shares your life
please save some time for me.
Though others all will come and go
I'm always your forever friend.

Let Me Live

I'm not even born yet
so, why do you hate me?
Don't blame me for somebody else's error.
Let me live!
Please allow me that right.
Don't destroy me before I have a chance to BE.

Let me see the world and feel my life.
Allow me to exist.
Permit me to belong;
if not to you, then to another.

Don't deny my right to life and laughter.
Let me touch the sky and taste the wind.
Allow me to dream and find desires.
Permit me to give,
and most of all, to love.

How do I know whether I'll be no-one or greatness
if you destroy me before I am born?
Let me discover what my destiny is,
the legacy I may leave.
Please don't decide it for me
before I'm even born...

Something's Missing

Something's missing
and somehow you don't understand.
I just can't work it out.
Please tell me what is missing?
That thing that we once had
now buried in the sand,
eaten by the hungry blue-green sea.
How I wish I know what's missing.
Why don't you ever feel
the emptiness that's always behind us
or could it be, you just don't like to listen?
The other kids all worship you
but what they see I just don't know,
'cause I know you and all you try to be.
You're a simple minded person,
a make-believe pretender.
You should have been a star upon the stage.
That special something's missing
and I know that we won't find –
at least not while I'm near.
But you insist I stay
at least for one more day.
But I don't think that I can take it
'cause you're always trying to fake it
and I realize by now
that it's no use trying to beat it.
You've got to try to fool it
before you have a hope of getting free.
So, I think it's time for you to go
and leave me for a while at least
'cause I'm not your little baby anymore.
I've grown into a lady
with a real great friend who helps me
and he says that he'll be over very soon.
SO, mum it's time to let go

'cause dad, I have to get out
and try to make a life all for myself.
I wish it didn't happen
at least not the way it did.
'Cause it hurt me oh, so much.
But it really did convince me
that I had to say goodbye
'Cause something's missing
and I'd hate to see you cry.

* First published in 'SPECTRUM, An International Poetry Anthology', 1982

Dancing With Dragons

Oh, what a tangled web we live.
Ghosts of the past
dwell in the pockets
of today's garments.

One, two, three, step, two, three,
come dance with me and my pain.
One, two, three, turn, two, three,
come dance with me and my shame.

Moments of rejection
rise up to taunt me,
bitter betrayals
chase and haunt me.

One, two, three, slide, two, three,
come dance with me and despair.
One, two, three, dip, two, three,
come dance with me and my fear.

Invisible boundaries
limit my choices,
guide my steps,
cloud my dreams.

Come dance with me and my dragons
Let us lead you in the dance to freedom.
Feel the healing of spirit.
Experience the power of dancing with dragons.

This Isn't About You

You think you're unique
but you're just like everyone else.
You're weak, so weak.
But this isn't about you.

It's just some words strung together
about someone I used to know.
A person from my past.
Someone with a big ego.

Thanks for your time,
for the moments we shared,
but I'm glad we're through.
Thanks for the bullet I've been spared.

Not everything is about you.
I know you wish it was.
The world doesn't revolve around you.
This isn't about you.

I know you'll think it is,
but this isn't about you.
Think what you want,
but if the shoe fits…

Silence

Don't want to live in silence anymore.
Been living outside my truth,
feelings shut behind the door,
stifled deep inside my core.

Want to shout to the hills,
let the honesty pour out,
avoid this clash of wills,
put an end to doubt.

always in fear
of causing offence,
saying what they want to hear.
Silence makes no sense.

No more doormat,
mild and meek.
A more assertive hat
is the flavour I seek.

Staying silent to keep the peace
gets me nowhere.
Need to find my voice.
Opinions are permitted to share.

I Know

I know a place called pain.

I know a place called loneliness.

I know a place filled with emptiness;
numbness, every minute of every day.

I know a place called depression.

It's where I live.

These Pills

Numb to excitement,
feeling no awe,
no sense of wonderment
immune to it all.

Stifled and smothered,
dumbed down, muffled,
lacking motivation,
wearing a mental frown.

Lifeless and dull,
flat and withdrawn,
detached and muted
These pills are taking my spark.

People talk at me
but all I hear is words.
My mind is in over-drive
but no thoughts are taking shape.

'Give a fuck' meter at zero,
I can't get involved,
interaction at an all-time low.
These pills are stealing my spirit.

Spare A Thought

Spare a thought for the walking wounded,
pause and pray for the outcasts.

Take a breath and look around,
view the crowds of misfits.

Spare a thought for the walking wounded.
Add my name to the list.

Potential

You had the potential for everything
but I never knew you.
You could have opened doors to greatness
but you never touched them.
You held the keys to the future
but you never used them.
You were the focus of my loving
but you never knew me.

You were never born
but you were everything.
I knew you better than anyone
yet I never knew you at all.

Why?

Why is it that so many people are only happy...
when they are unhappy?

It Comes At Night

It comes at night.
After a day spent ignoring it,
it slams into me
in the quiet before sleep.

This overwhelming emptiness,
this acute loneliness,
a sense of utter futility
and absolute helplessness.

With total lack of reason
it eats me, devours me
until I beat it down,
crush it into submission
so I can wake
and start anew.

Bruises

Bruises heal
but cruel words leave scars.

Intensive Care

Teather my heart
don't let it float away,
keep my feet on the ground.
Love in overdrive.

Cradle my heart
mend it with kindness,
lead my steps forward.
Love in intensive care.

I Knew You Better

I knew you better than anyone,
yet I never knew you at all.
You held all my love
but you never met me.
So many hopes for you,
so many dreams.
Hopes and dreams unfulfilled.
No-one knew you.
You never got to live.

Reach For Me

Cold little child,
so cold, so sad little child.
Don't hide your heart away from me.
I'll give you love, please reach for me.

Huddled in your blackness,
I try to bring you light
to pull you from the darkness.
Everything can be all right.

You're safe within your dreams,
a world of smiles and laughter
where no-one tries to hurt you
and no-one chases after.

Your world is cold and empty,
devoid of life and meaning.
You've let a wall enclose your mind
and it's stopped your heart from healing.

I wrap my arms around you.
You don't even know I'm there.
I bring your favourite flowers
but all you do is stare.

I wake to find you trembling
in the corner by the window.
There's a man who's here to get you.
Where he is you do not know.

How can my love help you
when the world outside's not there?
Your world is trapped within you.
Let me in, I've love to share.

But wait, your eyes are shining!
Your cheeks are blessed with tears.
Keep crying little child
and give me all your fears.

A Blessing

May angels hold your hand when you sleep,
fairies be at watch over your shoulder while you are awake,
and may you have the fiercest dragon at your back in times of
hardship.

Good Morning

Good Morning
Welcome to a new day.
Good Morning
Here's to a fresh start.
Here's to a day worth waking up for.
Yesterday is been and gone.
Today is here for the taking.
Seize the moment.
Today is a blessing.
Today is a gift.

I Wish

I wish there could be no more sadness,
no more poverty,
no more hunger.
I wish there could be no more heartbreak,
no more hatred,
no more racism.
I wish there was no more cancer,
no more illness,
no more hurt.
I wish there could be no more judgement,
no more bigotry,
no more repression.
I wish we could all live in harmony,
in love, happiness, and kindness.
I wish we could all live in peace.

Why Don't You Believe?

You're beautiful inside and out.
You're smart and clever.
You're kind and generous,
but why don't you believe it?

People tell you all the time
that you're wonderful,
you're funny and witty,
but why don't you believe it?

Everyone knows
you're amazing and special.
You're one in a billion,
but why don't you believe it?

Myself Divided

The me I am with you
is different
to the me I am at work
or with my family.
Multi-faceted me;
different with everyone,
different in every situation.
I'm the same
but different.
Myself divided.

One Moment

One moment
can change your entire life.
One moment
can become the future.

One moment leads to the next
then the next,
then a whole chain of moments
becomes history.

One moment
can be the most important of your life.
One moment
can change everything.

I Hide

I hide behind a smile.
I hide behind a joke.
I hide behind platitudes.
I hide behind an invisible wall.
I hide from the world.
I hide, I hide.

I'm Me

I'm not 'sick'
or 'deviant'.
I don't need to be 'fixed'.
I'm not broken.
I'm not 'wrong'.
I'm not normal.
I'm different.
I'm unique.
I'm not the same as you.
I'm spicy.
I'm me.

Worst Hero Ever

I'm not brave
or heroic.
I'm never at the right place
at the right time.
I'm not courageous.
I don't rescue people in peril.
I don't prevent disasters.
I can't run fast,
soar high,
or stop a speeding bus.
I've never killed a vampire
or saved the world.
No superpowers.
I'm not invincible.
I'm not immortal.
I'm the worst hero ever!

A Blessing

May angels hold your hand when you sleep,
fairies be at watch over your shoulder while you are awake,
and may you have the fiercest dragon at your back in times of
hardship.

About The Author

Caron Carr lives in Australia with ASD, a gaming console, and two cats, Shanti, and Rocket. The cats are great at hugs and listening but, as it turns out, are terrible editors.

In her youth, she wanted to join the boy scouts, be Prime Minister, and work for National Geographic. None of these dreams came true but many others have.

Her favorite color is sparkle.